IBERT

HISTOIRES FOR ONE PIANO, FOUR HANDS

EDITED BY MAURICE HINSON AND ALLISON NELSON

AN ALFRED MASTERWORK EDITION

Cover art: The Cliff Walk (1882)
by Claude Monet (1840–1926)
Courtesy of Corel Professional Photos

JACQUES IBERT

HISTOIRES (FOR ONE PIANO, FOUR HANDS)

Edited by Maurice Hinson and Allison Nelson

Contents

About This Edition

This authoritative edition is a compilation of five duets, originally published separately by Leduc in 1922. Ibert's original pedal markings are indicated. Additional editorial pedaling is enclosed in parentheses. Ibert's fingerings appear in italics; all others are editorial. All parenthetical material is editorial.

About the Composer and the Music

Jacques Ibert was born on August 15, 1890 in Paris, France, and died in the same city in 1962. He studied with Gabriel Fauré (1845–1924) and Paul Vidal (1863–1931) and won the Prix de Rome in 1919. From 1937 to 1955, he was director of the French Academy in Rome, Italy. Ibert composed ballets, chamber and piano music, operas, songs and symphonic poems. His polished writing displays characteristics of Neoclassical and Impressionistic styles and is frequently witty and light.

The music in this edition comes from a collection of 10 pieces entitled *Histoires* (Stories), composed in 1922. Ibert arranged five of the pieces for piano duet. The pictorial effects of these pieces demonstrate Ibert's ability to develop musical pictures in snapshot form, as well as his talent for blending transparent and strongly shaped ideas in a simple way.

La meneuse de tortues d'or (The Girl Leading the Golden Turtles).[1] This calm, melancholic movement features a flowing melody with sparse supporting chords. Its gentle coda closes with three majestic chords.

Form: Binary (**A B** coda). **A** = measures 1–35; **B** = 36–72; coda = 73–89.

Le petit âne blanc (The Little White Donkey). This piece originated during a 1922 trip to Tunisia, where Ibert encountered a little white donkey. This humorous, charming piece is a delightful staccato study. Both the title and the music provide clues to assist the pianists in realizing a possible story. The staccato 16th notes in the beginning suggest the constant trotting of the little donkey from afar (*lointain*, in the distance). The 32nd / dotted-16th note figures, which first appear in measures 11–14 of the primo part, might represent the donkey's "hee-haws." Other versions of these "hee-haws" are heard in the primo part at measures 25–27, 34–37 and 42–45. The mood changes quickly at measure 30, and suddenly the little donkey begins to move more quickly. In her discussion of this piece, Celia Mae Bryant suggests that the driver cracks the whip at measure 30 to urge the little donkey onward.[2] The offbeat accents in measures

46–53 could represent the donkey stumbling while slowing down. The opening mood returns (even more softly) in measure 54, and the final destination is reached at measure 84 as the sound of trotting fades into the distance and then stops.

Form: Ternary (**A B A**[1] coda). **A** = measures 1–29; **B** = 30–53; **A**[1] = 54–80; coda = 81–84.

A Giddy Girl. This piece was inspired by a dance Ibert had with an English girl, who began to faint in the composer's arms. As indicated in the score (at measure 1), the piece is written "in the style of a sentimental English romance." The "giddy girl" is quite fickle; her changeable emotions are depicted through numerous tempo and character changes: measures 1–3 = opening tempo; 4 = a little held back; 5–8 = *a tempo*; 9–16 = a little slower; 17–18 = slow down and diminish; 19–21 = *a tempo*; 22 = a little held back; 23–30 = *a tempo*. It seems as though she just can't make up her mind. Her coquettish nature is what this capricious little piece is all about. The ending in G major suggests that she is happy after all.

Form: Ternary (**A B A**[1]). **A** = measures 1–8; **B** = 9–18 (using material from the **A** section in different keys); **A**[1] = 19–30 (similar to the **A** section with left-hand chromatic figuration in measures 19–20 and 23–26).

La cage de cristal (The Crystal Cage). This piece suggests the dual image of a bird in a cage, as well as a fish in a bowl. Contrasting pianistic touches found in legato and staccato techniques become the focus of the piece, as Ibert provides chirping bird sounds through the use of grace notes, and an image of a swimming fish through the use of ascending and descending scale patterns.

Form: Ternary (**A B A**[1]). **A** = measures 1–8; **B** = 9–20; **A**[1] = 21–32.

Le cortège de Balkis (The Procession of Balkis). This piece was inspired by the Biblical story in I Kings 10, in which there is a brief account of the Queen of Sheba (also known as Balkis) traveling in a great procession to visit King Solomon. The music suggests the glory of a royal procession, with its elegant, majestic quality. Marked rhythms persist throughout. The piece closes the set with a pianissimo ending.

Form: Ternary (**A B A**[1] coda). **A** = measures 1–12; **B** = 13–35; **A**[1] = 36–43; coda = 44–47.

---

[1] This information comes from the forthcoming book, *Jacques Ibert* by Wesley Roberts.

[2] Celia Mae Bryant, "Teaching *The Little White Donkey*," *Clavier.* 12:5 (May–June 1970): 38–41.

I. La meneuse de tortues d'or

(The Girl Leading the Golden Turtles)

SECONDO

Jacques Ibert
(1890–1962)

ⓐ The unconnected "tie" is an indication to let the note ring.

I. La meneuse de tortues d'or

(The Girl Leading the Golden Turtles)

PRIMO

Jacques Ibert
(1890–1962)

ⓑ The unconnected "tie" is an indication to let the note ring.

Un peu lent et majestueux

II. Le petit âne blanc
(The Little White Donkey)

SECONDO

Avec une tranquille bonne humeur (♩ = ca. 84)

très léger

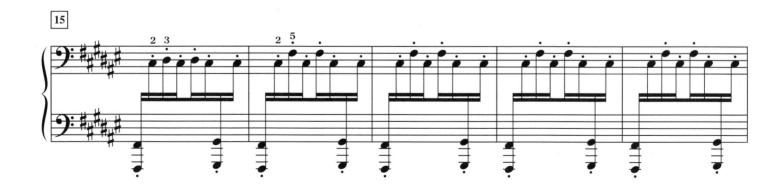

II. Le petit âne blanc
(The Little White Donkey)

PRIMO

en exagérant un peu les accents

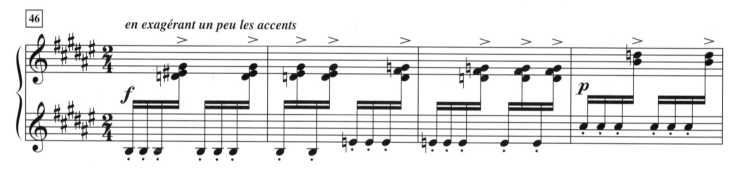

Un peu ralenti

(a tempo)
très léger

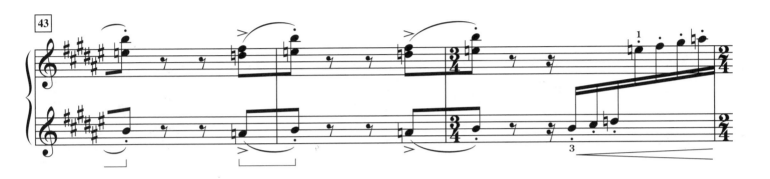

en exagérant un peu les accents

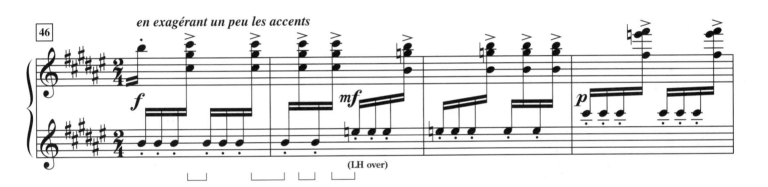

Un peu ralenti

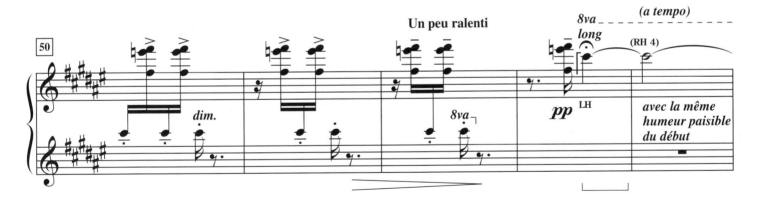

avec la même
humeur paisible
du début

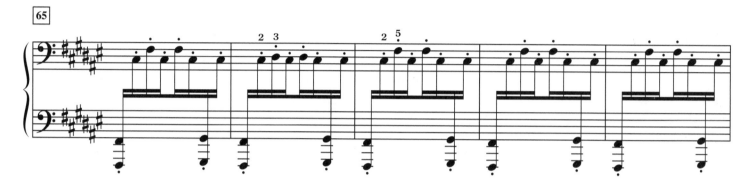

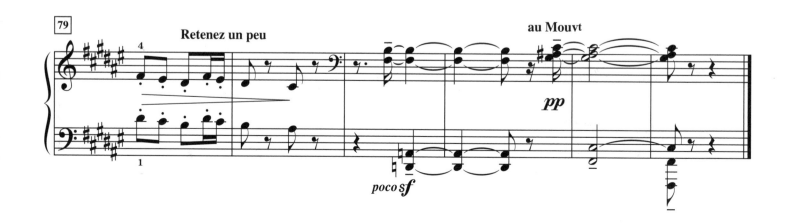

III. A Giddy Girl

SECONDO

III. A Giddy Girl

PRIMO

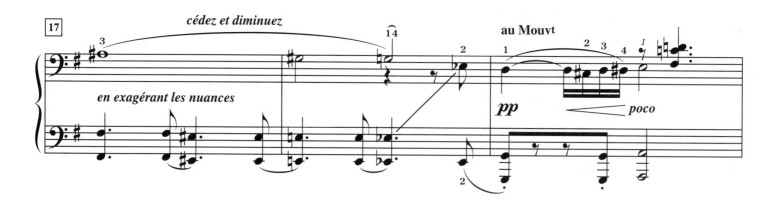

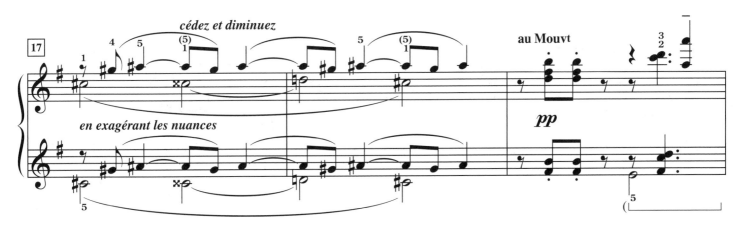

IV. La cage de cristal
(The Crystal Cage)

SECONDO

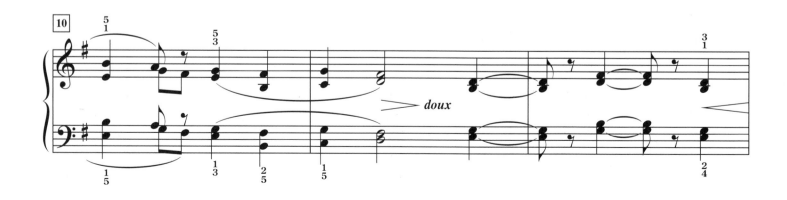

IV. La cage de cristal
(The Crystal Cage)

PRIMO

Un peu vite (♩ = ca. 116)

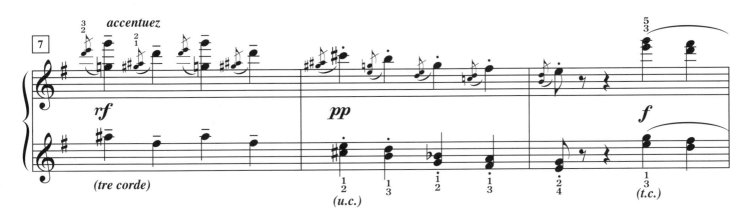

V. Le cortège de Balkis

(The Procession of Balkis)

SECONDO

V. Le cortège de Balkis

(The Procession of Balkis)

PRIMO

31

Retenez un peu

Commencez en dessous du mouvement pour animer progressivement

35

38

42

Vite

toujours **pp** *et piqué*

45

sec

Glossary of French Terms

Following is a glossary of French terms that can be found throughout the score of Ibert's *Histoires*.

accentuez – accent

allant – moving, going, stirring

au mouvt (au mouvement) – at the original tempo

avec la même humeur paisible du début – with the same quiet humor as the beginning

avec une tranquille bonne humeur – with a quiet good humor

cédé, cédez – yield, slow down

commencez en dessous du mouvement pour animez progressivement – begin below the tempo and speed up gradually

dans un mouvement libre et brillant – in a free and sparkling tempo

dans un rythme de danse souple et nonchalant – in a flexible and casual dance rhythm

dans un style de romance sentimentale anglaise – in a sentimental romantic English style

détaché – detached, separated

diminuez – (dim.) gradually becoming softer

doux – sweet and gentle

effacé – subdued, hidden, veiled

en augmentant – becoming louder, broader

en badinant – playfully

en exagérant – exaggerating

en pesant – heavily

en pressant jusqu'à la fin – hurrying toward the end

encore – still more, again

et – and

expressif – expressively, with emotion

gai – merry, gay

le thème en dehors – (the theme above) bring out the theme

léger – light, airy

lent – slow

lentement – slowly

les accents – the accents

les nuances – the dynamics

lointain – from a distance, remote

long – drawn out

majestueux – majestic

mélancolique – melancholy

moins – less

peu à peu – little by little

piqué – pick at the notes, very short

plus – more

ralenti – slowing down

retenez – hold back

retenu – held back

sec – dry, short and without pedal

soudain – suddenly

souple et gracieux – flexible and gracious

soutenu – sustained

toujours – always

très – very

un peu – a little

vite – fast, quick